FRANCIS FRITH'S
TOWN & CITY
MEMORIES

HITCHIN

SIMON WALKER has lived in Hertfordshire all his life. Born in Hitchin in 1950, he was educated at a local grammar school. After a career in computing and security Simon retired in 1999 to concentrate on local history. His other books include 'The Bridewells of Hitchin' and 'Hitchin Underground'. His only regret is that his chosen subject does not allow much scope for a sense of humour.

WALSWORTH ROAD 1901 46640

FRANCIS FRITH'S
TOWN & **CITY**
MEMORIES

HITCHIN

SIMON WALKER

FRANCIS FRITH'S
TOWN&CITY
MEMORIES

First published as Hitchin, A Photographic History of your Town
in 2001 by Black Horse Books, an imprint of The Francis Frith Collection®
Revised edition published in the United Kingdom in 2005 by
The Francis Frith Collection as Hitchin, Town and City Memories

Limited hardback edition ISBN 1-84589-068-X

Paperback edition ISBN 1-84589-041-8

British Library Cataloguing in Publication Data

Hitchin
Town and City Memories
Simon Walker

The Francis Frith Collection®
Frith's Barn, Teffont,
Salisbury, Wiltshire SP3 5QP
Tel: +44 (0) 1722 716 376
Email: info@francisfrith.co.uk
www.francisfrith.co.uk

FRANCIS FRITH'S
TOWN *&* CITY
MEMORIES

CONTENTS

THE MAKING OF AN ARCHIVE

F rancis Frith, Victorian founder of the world-famous photographic archive, was a devout Quaker and a highly successful Victorian businessman. By 1860 he was already a multi-millionaire, having established and sold a wholesale grocery business in Liverpool. He had also made a series of pioneering photographic journeys to the Nile region. The images he returned with were the talk of London. An eminent modern historian has likened their impact on the population of the time to that on our own generation of the first photographs taken on the surface of the moon.

Frith had a passion for landscape, and was as equally inspired by the countryside of Britain as he was by the desert regions of the Nile. He resolved to set out on a new career and to use his skills with a camera. He established a business in Reigate as a specialist publisher of topographical photographs.

Frith lived in an era of immense and sometimes violent change. For the poor in the early part of Victoria's reign work was a drudge and the hours long, and ordinary people had precious little free time. Most had not travelled far beyond the boundaries of their own town or village. Mass tourism was in its infancy during the 1860s, but during the next decade the railway network and the establishment of Bank Holidays and half-Saturdays gradually made it possible for the working man and his family to enjoy holidays and to see a little more of the world. With characteristic business acumen, Francis Frith foresaw that these new tourists would enjoy having souvenirs to commemorate their days out. He began selling photo-souvenirs of seaside resorts and beauty spots, which the Victorian public pasted into treasured family albums.

Frith's aim was to photograph every town and village in Britain. For the next thirty years he travelled the country by train and by pony and trap, producing fine photographs of seaside resorts and beauty spots that were keenly bought by millions of Victorians.

THE RISE OF FRITH & CO

Each photograph was taken with tourism in mind, the small team of Frith photographers concentrating on busy shopping streets, beaches, seafronts, picturesque lanes and villages. They also photographed buildings: the Victorian and Edwardian eras were times of huge building activity, and town halls, libraries, post offices, schools and technical colleges were springing up all over the country. They were invariably celebrated by a proud Victorian public, and photo souvenirs – visual records – published by F Frith & Co were sold in their hundreds of thousands. In addition, many new commercial buildings such as hotels, inns and pubs were photographed, often because their owners specifically commissioned Frith postcards or prints of them for re-sale or for publicity purposes.

In order to gain some understanding of the scale of Frith's business one only has to look at the catalogue issued by Frith & Co in 1886: it runs to some 670 pages. By 1890 Frith had created the greatest specialist photographic publishing company in the world, with over 2,000 stockists! The picture on page 7 shows the Frith & Co display board on the wall of the stockist at Ingleton in the Yorkshire Dales (left of window). Beautifully constructed with a mahogany frame and gilt inserts, it displayed a dozen scenes. The ever-popular holiday postcard we know today took many years to appear, and F Frith & Co was in the vanguard of its development. Postcards became a hugely popular means of communication and sold in their millions. Frith's company took full advantage of this boom and soon became the major publisher of photographic view postcards.

Francis Frith died in 1898 at his villa in Cannes, his great project still growing. His sons Eustace and Cyril continued their father's monumental task, expanding the number of views offered to the public and recording more and more places in Britain, as the coasts and countryside were opened up to mass travel. The archive Frith

created continued in business for another seventy years. By 1970 it contained over a third of a million pictures of 7,000 cities, towns and villages. The massive photographic record Frith has left to us stands as a living monument to a special and very remarkable man.

This book shows Hitchin as it was photographed by this world-famous archive at various periods in its development over the past 150 years. Every photograph was taken for a specific commercial purpose, which explains why the selection may not show every aspect of the town landscape. However, the photographs, compiled from one of the world's most celebrated archives, provide an important and absorbing record of your town.

INTRODUCTION

The Hertfordshire market town of Hitchin lies in a gap in the Chiltern Hills, a short distance from the border with Bedfordshire. The town is sited on the banks of the river Hiz, which runs through the town centre. Nikolaus Pevsner described Hitchin as being, after St Albans, 'the most visually satisfying town in the county'.

The area has been occupied for thousands of years. Stone and bronze implements are not uncommon, and there is ample evidence of Roman settlements throughout the area. Following the fall of the Roman Empire, the embryonic Hitchin found itself caught between the Romano-Britons and the Saxons, and was later involved in the Danish campaign of plunder. It was in about AD 600 that the town acquired its name: Hicce, after the Saxon tribe that dominated the area. By the time of the Norman Conquest Hicce was a possession of the Crown, and passed into the hands of William I: 'Rex Willelm tenet Hiz', says Domesday. The township comprised five hides (a hide was about 120 acres), with three mills, and woodland to feed six hundred pigs. There was also a monastery, which had extensive holdings.

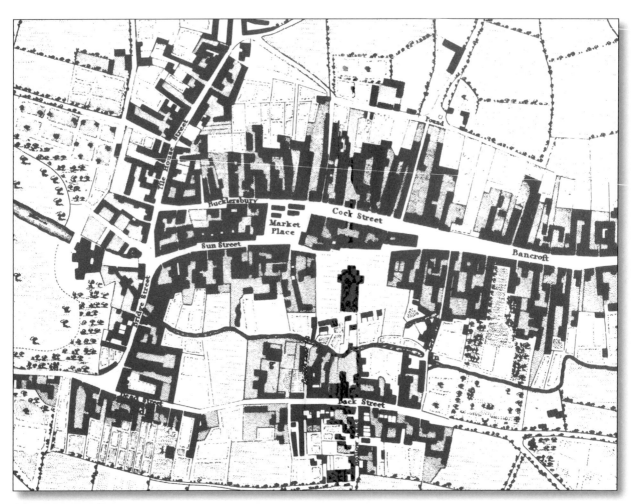

HITCHIN IN 1820

Brand Street was little more than a footpath, and Hermitage Road did not exist at all. Cock Street was to become the High Street, and Back Street and Dead Street combined to form Queen Street.

INTRODUCTION

Hitchin has long had a thriving market, and it was the market that had a major influence on the town's development. The older part of Hitchin is typical of an English market town: long and narrow, with areas that were once covered by traders' stalls now in-filled with timber-framed buildings.

In 1317, the Carmelite Order established a monastery in the town, and a few years later the Gilbertines followed suit. The town's prosperity began more and more to rely upon wool, and the wealth it generated can be seen in the parish church of St Mary, said to be the largest in the county. With Henry VIII's dissolution of the monasteries, the Carmelite and Gilbertine priories fell into private hands.

The next three hundred years were quiet ones for Hitchin; Even the Civil War failed to have a major impact. The townspeople got on with their day-to-day lives, and the town grew steadily. By the 1840s, the population had reached almost 8,000, and overcrowding became a serious problem. Sanitation was poor, and the water supply frequently contaminated. In 1850, the town formed a Local Board of Health, one of the first towns in the country to do so. Unfortunately, the plans and estimates for sewers and water supply were optimistic, and the Board became defunct in 1858. Hitchin was in the unique position of having no local government for the next fifteen years!

1850 also saw the arrival of the Great Northern Railway in Hitchin, a further spur to the town's growth and prosperity. Its status as a centre for the trading of grain was enhanced and, as the 20th century dawned, its leading citizens had no cause to view the future with anything but optimism. The two World Wars did little physical damage to the town, though many who fought for their country did not return. Like most of our market towns, following the Second World War, a period of development resulted in the destruction of some outstanding buildings. Progress was the key word, and for many people progress meant functional, box-like structures, often jarringly unsympathetic with older styles. Fortunately, much of the town's unique historic centre has survived, making Hitchin a pleasure to visit, for the historian and the shopper alike.

But for how long remains to be seen - development tends to be piecemeal, without consideration of an overall plan; it creeps up unnoticed, and architectural gems are picked off one by one. Before anyone realises what has happened, the history and character of a town can be destroyed forever.

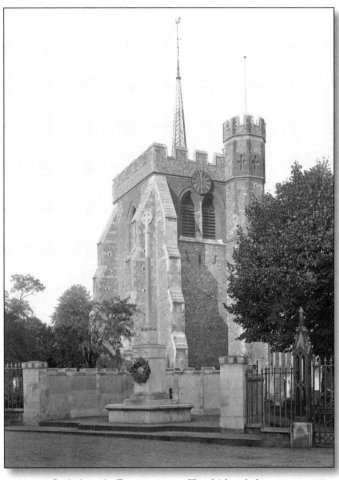

ST MARY'S CHURCH AND THE WAR MEMORIAL 1931
84195

A view of St Mary's Church in 1931, with the War Memorial in the foreground. In 1752, the Revd William Cole wrote that the tower was: 'one of the most clumsy and heavy ones I ever saw'. Perhaps 'solid' is a kinder description.

THE MARKET PLACE

Hitchin has held a market since the 12th century, and probably well before then. The township was a royal manor, and the Crown retained the market tolls, so it was in the monarch's interest to ensure that trading continued. In addition to the market, held every Tuesday, there were fairs twice a year. The early markets and fairs were not as we know them now. A large proportion of the goods traded were livestock and produce: horses, cattle, sheep, pigs and fowl; as well as grain, vegetables and dairy products, leatherwork and straw plait. The fairs were three-day events, and an excuse for general festivity. Nor was the market confined to the Market Place; it once ran from Bancroft to Tilehouse Street. All sorts of characters were part of a normal market day. In addition to the traders, there were dancers and tumblers, peddlers and hagglers, thieves, rogues and vagabonds - all trying to eke out a precarious living. Quack doctors plied their trade, selling dubious potions and pulling teeth. Amidst the hustle and bustle, the parish constable checked weights and measures, and the aletaster monitored the quality of the ale. A 'Pie Powder' court (from the French 'pieds poudre', or dusty feet) tried disputes with itinerant traders. The town stocks were conveniently sited

THE MARKET PLACE

THE MARKET 1901 46633

This photograph shows how the traffic used to run diagonally across the Market Place. To the left of the Italianate Corn Exchange, G C Flanders advertises the various cycles sold in the shop: Swift, Rover, Royal Enfield, Rudge and Whitworth amongst them. On the other side of the Exchange is Edwin Logsdon's confectionery business. Gatward's Engineers are to the right of this, and on the roof next door a man seems to be painting the chimneystack. On the far right is the Red Cow, and to its left is the Post Office. Next comes John R Jackson's, a milliner and outfitter. In the right foreground, a policeman keeps an eye on proceedings.

in the Market Place, the traditional site for punishment for centuries; in 1774, Elizabeth Parr was publicly whipped there for the theft of nutmeg. She was not the first, nor was she to be the last.

Priority at the market was given to local traders, and the trading opened only when the toller rang the bell in the purpose-built bell house. By 1829, the bell house was gone, and the church bells signalled the start of the trading. At about the same time pressure grew for a second trading day, which eventually led to the Saturday market, concentrating on goods rather than farming and agricultural produce. With their business done,

traders of all descriptions repaired to the local inns and alehouses to replenish their energies before starting on their long journey home. The Sun, the Red Cow and the Angel did a roaring trade on market days.

The arrival of the railway in 1850 increased the scale of trading, and in 1852 a competition with a prize of £50 was held for the design of a new corn exchange. William Beck, a local architect, submitted a design free of charge - it was after all a prestige project - and just eleven months later, on 22 March 1853, the building was formally opened. Initially, the Exchange was overshadowed by the Shambles, a ramshackle group of buildings which stood just to the southeast, in the Market Place: they were finally demolished in 1856. However, the Exchange's success was not to last, and the building was used for a number of purposes over the years, most recently a bar and restaurant.

Trading in the Market Place continued until World War II, when it moved to St Mary's Square. The Market Place became a car park, though part of it was covered by a large open water tank, for the fire brigade, should the town be bombed; fortunately it was not required. Following the war, the tank was removed and the motorcar re-established its rule. For many years, the traffic had flowed diagonally across the Market Place between the High Street and Sun Street, but as the pressure of traffic grew, a one-way system was introduced and the roads diverted around the square. The whole of the centre was given over to parking. This diversion was not without risk: many of the properties surrounding the open area have extensive cellars, reaching well beyond the boundaries of the buildings themselves. Some are very old - in a number of cases older than the current premises to which they belong. The danger of collapse was a real one, and as vehicles became larger and heavier, it became clear that something must be done. In 1993, the Market Place was refurbished, and some of its original character was reclaimed. A radar survey of the square revealed the danger points, and the roads moved to avoid them.

What about the buildings that surround the Market Place? The old Post Office is now a hairdressers, and of the licensed premises that once existed in the Market Place, only the Rose and Crown is still trading. This site has been a pub for many years - it is known for example that Stephen Papworth, the landlord, was refused his licence for heavy drinking, and that was in 1852. The Swan Inn, starting point for daily coaches to London and Hertford for so many years, closed in 1884; it had existed since at least 1539. The site became the Swan Ironworks, run by John Gatward who, by 1900, described his business as a 'complete house furnishers and general ironmongers'. In 1924, it became a shopping arcade, which it remains today. The shops along each side are the outhouses and stables of that once extensive tavern. The old Red Cow now sells electrical equipment.

The Gatward family maintains a presence in the Market Place with Gatward Jewellers, on the corner with Sun Street. The

MARKET PLACE 1922 71893

By 1922, new businesses had taken over many of the premises in the Market Place. On the left are Timothy Whites and Taylor's, a chemist chain, then the Corn Exchange. Next is the Hitchin Playhouse, a cinema that opened in 1913, advertising accommodation for 800 spectators. Gatward's is still there, but John Jackson's business has gone: replaced by the Midland Bank. The Post Office has transferred to Brand Street; Briggs & Co., the Leicester Boot Company with its impressive gilded sign, and the Maypole Dairy, share its old premises. In the centre of the picture, an open-topped bus picks up passengers next to a theatre billboard. The cart (right foreground) is loaded with what looks like animal hides.

MARKET PLACE C1955 H89025

This is the same view as on pages 12-13, in the mid 1950s. The Hitchin Playhouse has been replaced by Burtons tailors, the first floor of which houses the Lucania Temperance Billiards Hall. I Pirkis & Son, decorators' merchants, have replaced Gatward's. Parking places have been marked out, including no-parking areas: a sign of things to come.

THE MARKET PLACE

business is housed in delightful timber-framed premises, and is thought to be the oldest family jeweller in the county. Also on the south side, a few doors up from Gatward's, the bizarre Victorian Shilcock building attracts many a second glance.

Only the buildings on the east side of the square have been lost, to a 1970s development that is quite out of keeping with the area. George Spurr's drapery occupied the site for many years; the shop had a pneumatic tube system that used to carry the customer's bill and money to the cashier, who returned the bill with the appropriate change in the same manner. It was worth buying things in Spurr's just to watch them take your money. When the first edition of this book was published in 2001, the fate of the Churchgate Centre and Hitchin market were under discussion. Today, in 2005, and after two consultant's reports and numerous meetings with townspeople, the situation is unchanged. We still do not know what the future holds for the east side of the market place or the market itself. Only one thing is sure - everyone agrees that the Churchgate Centre should be replaced with something more in keeping with the historic character of the town.

Above: THE ARCADE 1931 84207

The Shopping Arcade has scarcely changed since this photograph was taken in 1931. The shops were once the outbuildings of the Swan Yard.

Market Place c1955 H89026

The Market Place in 1955 - this time looking towards the churchyard. Left to right: W T Barker, tailor, Maison Gerard, a 'costumier', owned by Gerard Ceunis (a First World War Belgian refugee), Halsey's grocery, the Rose and Crown and finally George Spurr, who made sure everyone knew his stock in trade.

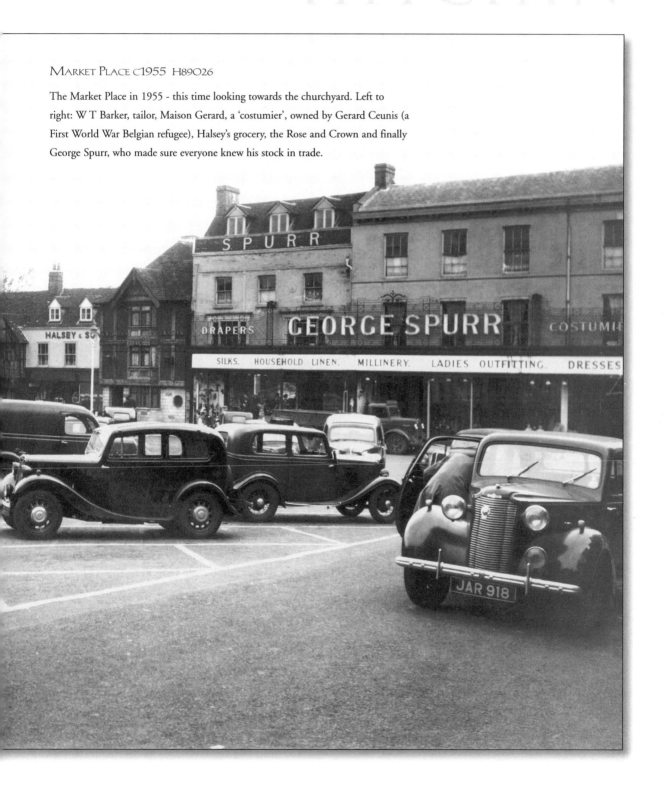

ORDNANCE SURVEY MAP

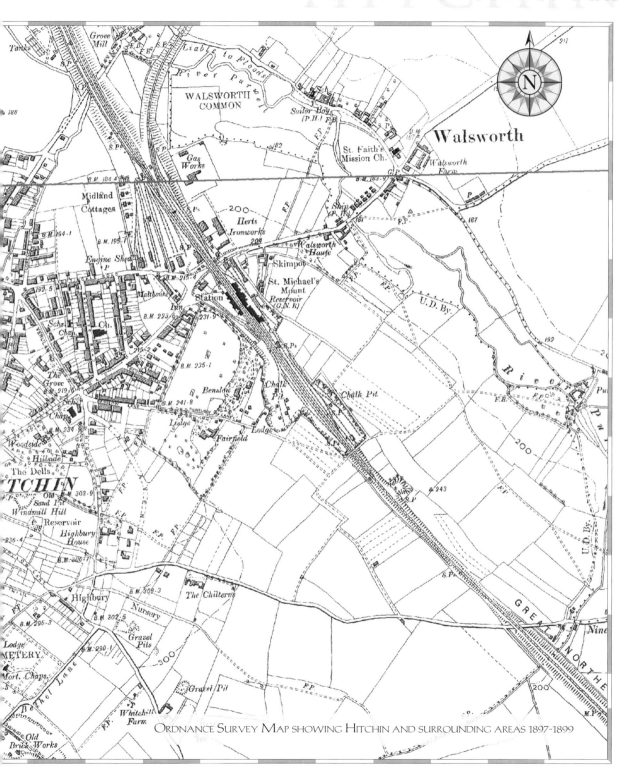

ORDNANCE SURVEY MAP SHOWING HITCHIN AND SURROUNDING AREAS 1897-1899

BUCKLERSBURY AND SUN STREET

SUN STREET c1955 H89053

In 1955, Sun Street was much the same as it is today. Faulkner's estate agents are on the left. Paternoster's stationery office is the building centre left, with its large sign between the first and second floors. On the right, we have W J Roberts, a shoe repairer, and next to him is Philpott's, the house furnisher. The two businesses are housed in a building that was once part of the Lucas brewery, founded in 1709. Next door, Mrs C M Astle's Hitchin Café advertises hot meals, served all day.

BUCKLERSBURY AND SUN STREET

BUCKLERSBURY AND SUN STREET

Above: THE SUN HOTEL c1965 H89301

In the 1960s, the Sun Hotel's yard did not include fire escapes from the upstairs rooms, as it does now. Otherwise, there is little but the parked cars to give a clue to the date of this photograph. The timber-framed buildings, on the left, are believed to date from the 16th century.

Right: THE SUN HOTEL c1965 H89504

A bedroom of the Sun Hotel as it was in 1965. Unfortunately guests no longer have the opportunity of sleeping in such grand beds.

Paternoster and Hales sold all sorts of stationery services and supplies, including artists' materials.

Bucklersbury and Sun Street run southwards from the Market Place. These old roads are lined with historic buildings, dating from the mid-15th century onwards. Timber-frame frontages with crooked roofs stand side-by-side with elegant Georgian and Victorian structures; the entrances to old inns lead into quiet yards flanked by stable buildings and outhouses.

Sun Street was once called Angel Street, after the Angel Inn, which carried a date of 1450 on its façade; the building was in fact much older. A wonderful old inn, it sadly became unstable when its 14th-century main roof beam broke, and it had to be demolished.

Long before the fall of the Angel, though, the Sun Hotel had usurped its place as the premier inn of Hitchin, and the street was renamed to reflect its dominance. A real coaching inn, the Georgian frontage gives little clue to what lies within and behind. Of particular interest is a false window painted onto the second floor façade.

The Royal Mail coach once stopped here to change horses, and to provide passengers with a brief respite before the continuation of their uncomfortable journey. At one time, the Sun raised its own animals, grew its own vegetables, and brewed its own beer. The Elizabethan yard is still to be seen, as is the fine assembly room, dating from 1770. Hitchin magistrates sat in judgement in the Sun for many years, whilst the Angel Inn next door was the home of the ecclesiastical court of the Archdeacon of Huntingdon.

On the other side of the road from the Sun Hotel is Paternoster's former printing office, clearly marked for all to see. The Paternoster family have been in Hitchin for centuries, as wagon masters, surveyors, printers, stationers and other trades besides.

Why Bucklersbury is so-called is something of a mystery. It may be connected with armourers or harness makers; the name has certainly been in use for more than 300 years. However, the road is much older. Two of Hitchin's oldest inns are to be found along it: the George and the Red Hart, both dating from the 15th century.

The George is the older of the two inns, but only by 20 years or so. Built as a merchant's house, it became an inn quite early: by 1676, it was known as the 'Faulcon'. In later years, it became the Beehive, and finally the George - not after a royal George, but after George Washington, whose secretary, the Revd William Gordon, was born in Hitchin. It is said that Royalist prisoners were

BUCKLERSBURY AND SUN STREET

held in the cellar of the Red Hart during the Civil War; it may be true: inns were often used for the confinement of prisoners, and they sometimes appeared in court too drunk to plead.

At the north end of Bucklersbury, almost opposite the George, are Hawkins outfitters, who have traded from Bucklersbury since 1863, expanding slowly along the road for more than a century. Just thirteen years after Hawkins founded his business, Tom Brooker opened his hardware store in Walsworth Road. Brooker opened a second shop in Bucklersbury in 1896, taking over vacant premises next door in 1937 and again in 1960.

THE RED HART HOTEL YARD 1931 84204

The Red Hart yard in 1931. The public and private bars are on the left. The barn at the end of the yard has been demolished, but otherwise there has been little change. It is claimed that this yard was the site of the last public hanging in Hitchin, though it must be said that there is little or no evidence to support this tradition.

BUCKLERSBURY AND SUN STREET

BUCKLERSBURY 1908 60875

Bucklersbury - looking towards the Market Place in 1908. The George Inn is on the left, and next door but one is Boxall's, a taxi firm still in business in Hitchin, though now from different premises. A door or two up is Tom Brooker's hardware shop. On the other side of the street is the Hitchin Dairy, and the draper nearest the camera is Hawkins.

TILEHOUSE, BRIDGE AND PARK STREETS

THE COOPER'S ARMS 1903 49745

The Cooper's Arms, just after the turn of the 20th century; McMullens advertise their 'fine ales and invigorating stout'. The road surface shows signs of cobbling from an earlier age.

TILEHOUSE, BRIDGE AND PARK STREETS

Tilehouse Street was named after the tile kilns that were once nearby. The name appears in the Court Rolls for 1460 as 'Tylehousestret', and it was the main route into Hitchin from the west, until 1983 - it was blocked off after the bypass was built, and none too soon. Tilehouse Street was the main road to Luton, and the heavy lorries endangered some of its fine old buildings.

The architecture fronting the street ranges from Tudor to Victorian; a good many of the buildings seem Georgian, but behind these façades, there often lie earlier structures. Timber-framed homes were not always as desirable as they are today, and new brick and stone frontages were frequently appended to earlier buildings.

Near the top of the hill is the Cooper's Arms, a 15th-century building with the remains of stone mullioned windows and a fine fireplace. The interesting cellar is now sealed off. There is reason to believe that the building was once much larger than it is today.

A little further up stands the home of George Chapman (1559-1634), an important playwright, poet and translator of his day, and a friend of William Shakespeare. Chapman fell out of favour with James I for a while and spent a short time in prison - a result of his involvement with the play 'Eastward Ho', which poked fun at the Scots. He is best remembered for his translations of the works of Homer.

From Tilehouse Street, Charlton Road once led towards the village of the same name. Though a tiny place, the village is of immense importance to the steel industry as the birthplace of Henry Bessemer, inventor of the Bessemer converter. Charlton Road was blocked at the same time as Tilehouse Street, and became part of Wratten Road East. Access to the village is now via the bypass.

The Priory, at the junction of Tilehouse Street, Bridge Street and Sun Street, was founded by the Carmelite order in 1317. From 1546, the Radcliffe family owned the estate for over 400 years, but it is now a conference centre.

Very little of the original monastery remains. The oldest part of the present building is the cloisters, dating from between 1420 and 1450. John Radcliffe built the house we now see in about 1775. For centuries, the Priory pond facing Tilehouse Street provided water for horses, nowadays it provides a home for ducks. No description of the Priory would be complete without mentioning the tunnels, said to run to various destinations in the town. Sadly, the stories are almost certainly a misinterpretation of a monastic drain that once ran down to the River Hiz.

OLD HOUSES, TILEHOUSE STREET 1931 84201

The corner of Tilehouse Street and Charlton Road in 1931. This fine building has been restored, and substantial wooden beams uncovered on the façade. In 1931 the streets were still lit by gas, as evidenced by the lamp on the left.

TILEHOUSE, BRIDGE AND PARK STREETS

TILEHOUSE STREET c1955 H89052

Tilehouse Street, from the junction with Sun Street in 1955.
The weather-boarded building on the right is Barham's
gunsmiths, closed down after legislation destroyed its
viability. The building is far older than it looks, and has a
continuous jetty and fine crown post roof timbers.

TILEHOUSE, BRIDGE AND PARK STREETS

TILEHOUSE STREET 1901 46639

TILEHOUSE, BRIDGE AND PARK STREETS

TILEHOUSE, BRIDGE AND PARK STREETS

Photograph 46639 (page 30-31) shows Tilehouse Street in 1901, looking west. Today, the street has hardly changed, although the Three Tuns on the left is now a private house. It used to be said that if a customer stumbled when negotiating the three steps into the pub, he was too drunk to be served; presumably stumbling on the way out was not the landlord's concern. Next door is a shop from which George Day sold handmade baskets until his death in 1955. Note the shop with the awnings over the first floor windows, in the centre of the picture; it is Sam Taylor's Hygienic Bakery, and all bread was advertised as being baked in a Baily-Baker hygienic hot-air oven.

Bridge Street runs from the Priory entrance eastwards. The road is named for the crossing of the river, a little-noticed bridge that bears a date of 1784. Before the bridge was built, the road was named Spittle Street, after the hospital and pest house that was once there. When new sewer pipes were laid in the 1980s the contractors came upon a thick layer of flint rubble, believed to be the remnants of a ford predating the road bridge. To supplement the ford, there was a footbridge for pedestrians.

All the buildings on the north side of the street, from the river to Sun Street, were once owned by Lucas's brewery, one of many maltings in the town. Much of the site was demolished in 1963. Several of the outstanding timber-framed buildings to the south were owned by the Radcliffe family, and formed part of the Priory estate.

CHARLTON, BRICK KILN LANE 1903 49746

Charlton was the birthplace of Henry Bessemer, inventor of the Bessemer converter.

TILEHOUSE, BRIDGE AND PARK STREETS

THE PRIORY C1955 H89007

The Priory as it appeared in 1955. The house looks
much the same today, though it is now a conference
centre. The bridge in the foreground is 18th century,
built of brick rubble with a moulded parapet.

TILEHOUSE, BRIDGE AND PARK STREETS

At the bottom of the lower end of Park Street, two hostelries stand side-by-side: the Half Moon Inn and Lister House Hotel (now the Lord Lister). George Buller ran the Half Moon in the late 19th century. His main passion was beekeeping. The Lister House Hotel stands on the site of Isaac Brown's Quaker Academy, which burned down in 1845. The hotel was named for Joseph Lister, the pioneer of antiseptic surgery, who was educated at the school for a while.

Park Street leads southward to Hitchin Hill, and in turn, to the old London Road. Until 1806, the hill was extremely steep from the Moorhens pub as far as a sharp right-hand bend. The Welwyn Turnpike Trustees decided that it was far too dangerous; indeed, it must have been in the days of horse-drawn traffic, so a substantial cutting was made, which is still in use today. The footpath has stayed where it was, though, and follows a route well above the road.

BRIDGE STREET C1955 H89045

Bridge Street, looking east. Sweet jars are clearly visible in Furr's window. Three doors up is J B Crone, a furniture dealer; next door, W H Walker sells cycles. At the top of the street stand the Lister Hotel and the Half Moon, looking onto the area known as 'the Triangle'. On the left is The Hill View Hotel, one of several Hitchin establishments that catered for cyclists. The building closest to us in the photograph has lintel supports and bargeboards, depicting dragons.

TILEHOUSE, BRIDGE AND PARK STREETS

PARK STREET 1901 46644

In 1901 the main road to the south was Park Street. The lane to the right leads to Gosmore, and at the top of the hill in front of us, hidden by the bushes, is the Moorhens public house. The footpath follows the original level of the road.

Tilehouse, Bridge and Park Streets

TILEHOUSE, BRIDGE AND PARK STREETS

BRIDGE STREET C1955 H89012

Bridge Street in about 1955, looking towards the junction of Tilehouse and Sun Streets. The sign next to H A Furr's confectionery shop advises traffic for Bedford and Luton to use Tilehouse Street, while traffic for Baldock is directed down Sun Street. The hump in the road by the Plough and Dial is the bridge, which gives the street its name. On the right is Sale's garage, with a Pratt's petrol pump delivering Shell fuel.

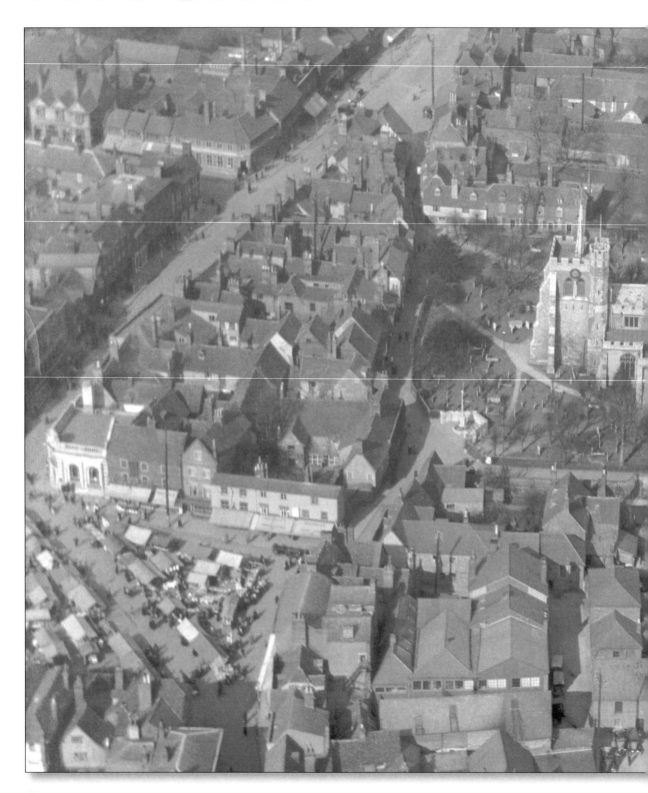

HITCHIN FROM THE AIR 1924 AF9819

ST MARY'S CHURCH 1931 84188

St Mary's from the northeast in 1931. This photograph gives a good impression of the size of the building. It is worthwhile walking around the outside of the church to view the gargoyles and corbels, some of which are amusing, others grotesque.

ST MARY'S CHURCH AND THE BIGGIN

ST MARY'S CHURCH 1903 49739

An atmospheric view of St Mary's south porch and tower, in 1903. The tower shows patches of cement rendering now removed.

St Mary's Church and the Biggin

The oldest of Hitchin's churches is St Mary's. It was originally dedicated to St Andrew, and stands in the centre of the town, to the west of the river Hiz. Development over many years has encroached upon the churchyard, which was originally much larger than it is today; burials have turned up as far away as Brand Street.

The existing church dates from the 12th century, erected on the site of an earlier Saxon building. Like most of Britain's houses of worship, additions and alterations have been made to it ever since, sometimes by design, and occasionally by necessity. Part of the building collapsed in 'a great wind' in 1115; in 1298, an earthquake did more damage, and in 1304, the roof fell in.

The nave is oriented east/west, with aisles to the north and south. The chancel is to the east, with chapels to the north and south of it. To the west stands the 13th-century tower, with its later buttresses. Roman tiles are built into the structure, and a double sundial dated 1660 supplements the clock. The dial is marked 'Anno Salvus', the year of salvation: a reference to the restoration of the monarchy following the Civil War. The tower is topped with a short steeple of a type known as a Hertfordshire spike - though not unique to the county, it is most commonly found here.

The 12th-century nave is the oldest identifiable part of the church, though the site is much older. Over the chancel arch is an unusual window, which is claimed to be evidence that there was once a central tower. The font has been in the church since at least 1470. It is decorated with twelve apostles, whose faces were hacked off by Puritan soldiers in the 17th century. The font cover is Victorian: a remarkable piece of work in its own right.

St Mary's Church, The Interior 1901 46647

The interior, looking east.

St Mary's Church and the Biggin

The Church c1965 H89082

The church from the southeast. Like most old buildings, St Mary's requires constant maintenance work. Here, scaffolding has been erected to allow repairs to be made to several parts of the aisles and chapels. The buildings to the left are Warner's Almshouses.

The north aisle was added in 1325, and the one on the south 20 years later. The north and south porches belong to the 15th century, as do the chancel and the chapels to the north and south of it. The door to the south porch is original, and at least 500 years old. At one time screens ran the full width of the church, but in 1776, the central portion was destroyed. However, the sections before the chapels remain. The south, or Angel Screen, is as fine as any in the country (there are over 170 angels in different parts of the church). The north screen is less remarkable, but a competent piece of work nonetheless.

A number of brasses lie in the floor of the south chapel, including that of Elizabeth Mattock who died on 6 September 1485. She is depicted in her shroud, giving an insight into burial customs of the time.

The north chapel steps lead down to the charnel house, built to house the bones disturbed by the 15th-century improvements. The charnel house is not open to the public, nor does it still contain the remains for which it was built.

According to local tradition, in the mid 17th century Parliamentarian soldiers were garrisoned in the building. They are usually held responsible for defacing the decoration of the font and other figures of the church, both interior and exterior, though some of the damage may have been carried out during the reformation, 100 years earlier. These mutilations apart, the church has survived the centuries remarkably well.

St Mary's Church Screen 1903 49740

The screen to the north chapel. Immediately above this viewpoint is part of the 14th-century roof that once covered the chancel.

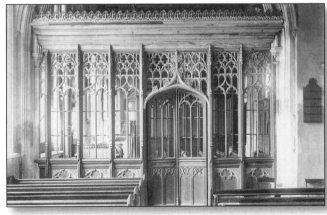

St Mary's Church and the Biggin

Iron railings once surrounded the churchyard to keep out the 'resurrection men', or body snatchers, who stole corpses to order for dissection by the medical profession. The railings were erected by public subscription following the theft of the body of Elizabeth Whitehead in 1828. Elizabeth was not the first victim, but the townsfolk were resolved that she should be the last. The railings were removed before the Second World War, and not during it as is sometimes suggested.

The burial ground surrounding St Mary's contains gravestones bearing a skull and crossbones motif. Some say that these memorials mark the last resting place of either plague victims or pirates, but neither explanation is true. This gruesome depiction of death was fashionable in the late 17th century, and can be found in many churchyards in England.

Businesses have come and gone in the Churchyard, but one of the most enduring was Halsey's. At one time or another, this old grocery concern occupied several premises between the Market Place and the Churchyard. As one of the most picturesque views in Hitchin, this short side road is also the most photographed.

Photograph 81716 (page 48) shows the same view of the Churchyard as the photograph on the right, but in 1929. The gates have been removed, and the memorial erected to the Hitchin men killed in the First World War. Allsop's is still in business, now trading as 'Ye Olde Hosierie Shoppe', and has moved down the block. Their old premises have been refurbished, and the timber frames revealed. Opposite Allsop's is Melia's: a grocery chain. The whole of the visible part of Halsey's window is dedicated to Green's, including their sponges and chocolate jelly moulds.

The old vicarage of St Mary's stands in the southwest corner of the Churchyard. Much altered, the building now houses a bookshop and a teashop. During conversion work in 1927, a number of human bones were found, as well as a void extending from the cellar towards the church. Unfortunately, no further investigations seem to have been made, and the cellar is now concreted over.

The west and northwest sections of the Churchyard retain much of their charm, the buildings dating from the 16th to the 19th centuries. While none is individually outstanding, as a group they make a delightful boundary to the Churchyard.

St Mary's Church and the Biggin

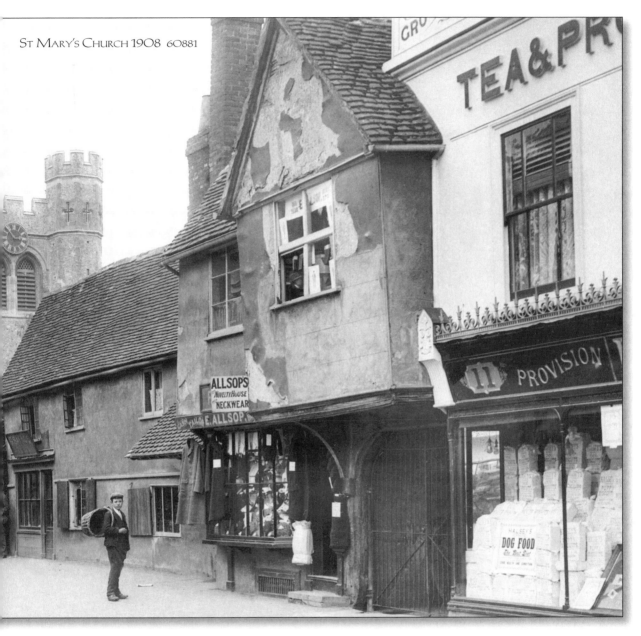

St Mary's Church 1908 60881

This 1908 view of the churchyard from the south shows the gates that once protected the dead from body snatchers. J Shipley Slipper, a dentist, held a surgery at Waldock's on the left, but only on alternate market days - a long wait if you'd just missed him. George Savage's draper's shop is by the gates on the right, and next door to him is Allsop's, trading as a cash tailor under the slogan: 'The Novelty House for Neckwear'. The façade of his shopfront has been rendered, and scoured with lines to give the impression that it is built of stone. Unfortunately, the years have taken their toll and the render is slowly falling off. Halsey's is on the right: an advertisement in the window draws attention to 'Halsey's Dog Food' - packets of puppy biscuits surround it. Strictly speaking, the buildings from Savage's to Halsey's are in the Market Place, whilst those on the other side are in the Churchyard.

St Mary's Church and the Biggin

Above: The Churchyard 1929 81716

The corner of the window has a mirror in it, and the photographer and his tripod are just visible in the reflection - the photographer, photographed.

Right: The Churchyard c1965 H89063

The Churchyard in about 1965. The War Memorial is on the left and left of centre is Halsey's. W Darby & Co, occupying the old St Mary's vicarage, is an electrical retailer. Next door is Woodbridge's, specialising in gentlemen's shoes. C W Morris on the right is a draper and ladies' outfitter. The weighing machine between Woodbridge and Morris's took one old penny, less than 1/2p. Weighing machines like this one were once common, and an example can be seen in Hitchin Museum in Paynes Park.

ST MARY'S CHURCH AND THE BIGGIN

To the south east of the graveyard stand Warner's Almshouses. They stand upon the site of earlier cottages that were administered by the overseers of the poor, until 1761. In that year, Daniel Warner paid for them to be rebuilt. They were again rebuilt and enlarged with funds left by Elizabeth Lucas in 1893. From Miss Lucas's bequest the six inhabitants received 11s 5d each month.

On the east side of the River Hiz is The Biggin, originally a Gilbertine religious house founded by the lord of the manor, Edward de Kendale, in 1361. The tomb covers of Edward and his wife Elizabeth are preserved in the north aisle of St Mary's Church.

The Gilbertine order was founded in the 12th century, and was based on the Benedictine rule. The life was hard, with little contact with the outside world. Beauty and comfort were shunned, and the day spent in prayer and contemplation. The Biggin was surrendered to the Crown in 1538. Extensive rebuilding work was carried out in around 1585, but some of the original timberwork still survives in the roof, and there is evidence that parts of the old priory church structure were re-used in the southern wall.

By 1635, The Biggin had become a school run by Joseph Kempe, whose will provided for the care of 'ten poor ancient or middle aged women' in the building, as long as they had formerly been 'diligent in some honest calling'. Thus, the building became an almshouse. The number of inmates eventually rose to eighteen, and in 1960, the building was restored and updated.

From the High Street a pathway known as Aram's Alley runs through to the Churchyard. A much-respected teacher at the Church School in 1750, Eugene Aram was known in the town for his kindness to children and animals. No one suspected that he was on the run for murder; justice finally caught up with him in 1758 at King's Lynn, and he was hanged. His ghost is said to haunt the passageway that bears his name.

DETAIL OF H89063

St Mary's Church and the Biggin

St Mary's Church c1955 H89011

By the mid 1950s, Halsey's had taken over all the premises in the row, with the exception of a jewellers, James Walker. The billboard that was above the shop has been removed.

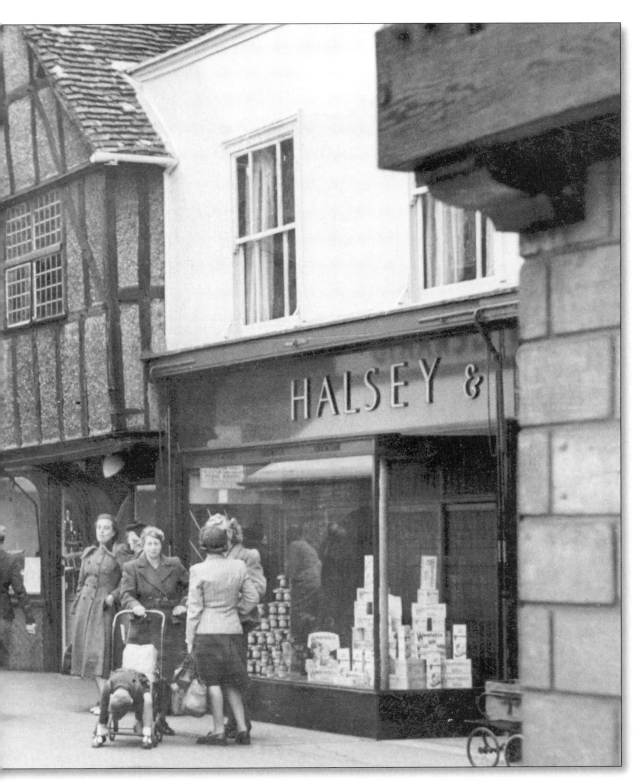

St Mary's Church and the Biggin

THE INNER COURTYARD OF THE BIGGIN 1903 49743

This view was taken in 1903, although it appears earlier. The timber colonnades are an unusual feature. The pump standing beneath the awning on the left was removed in 1960. On the right, a wooden water butt gathers rainfall, via a pipe from the guttering. At about this date, 18 needy women occupied the Biggin, receiving about 10s each.

St Mary's Church and the Biggin

Above: THE BIGGIN 1903 49742

This photograph of the Biggin was taken from the south in 1903. The section immediately before the camera is now demolished; nonetheless, what remains is a fascinating building. To the right of the picture is a pile of pipes, stored here temporarily during much needed refurbishment of Hitchin's sewer system.

Right: THE CHURCHYARD C1955 H89031

The view looking north in the Churchyard in the mid 1950s was much the same then as it is today. In 1963, a well was found in the premises facing us, then Wendy's Hat Shop. Believed to be early medieval, it was lined with a soft chalky stone, and contained 15 feet of clear water. A bakery now occupies the premises.

HIGH STREET AND BRAND STREET

THE HIGH STREET 1903 49736

This 1903 view looking south down the High Street is full of detail. It seems to have been taken one warm morning - note the open windows, and the summery dresses of the girls on the right. The Cock Hotel advertises a billiard table and stabling. A cast-iron milestone outside records the fact that it is 34 miles to London. Next to the Cock is Barclays Bank, built by Sharples, Exton and Lucas in 1841. Next-door-but-one to Barclays is the establishment of William Payne, an agricultural, veterinary and dispensing chemist. He was also a dentist, and advertised as 'the Hitchin Modern Pharmacy and Artificial Teeth Laboratory'. The road visible at the far side of the Market Place is Bucklersbury. Only one or two municipal gaslights are evident, but private ones supplement them: for example Wightman's, on the left, and B K Williams next door (drapers, silk mercers, costumiers, and milliners). The man on the left, in the road, is pushing a milk cart.

HIGH STREET AND BRAND STREET

From the Market Place, the High Street runs north to its junction with Brand Street. Both of these road names are relatively recent; the High Street was once Cock Street, and Brand Street was Pound Lane. The High Street is part of the long early-medieval market street of Hitchin, though none of the buildings of that period survive. The oldest survivor is the Cock Hotel, and though the date 1563 is recorded on the lintel support of the entrance, it may be as much as a hundred years older. The inn was once much larger than it is now; two thirds of the building was demolished in 1931 to make way for F W Woolworth's 3d and 6d Store. In 1964, Woolworth's sold the site to Boots, and bought a site further up the road. They demolished those buildings too, and erected their current shop. While not as pleasing to the eye as those that were knocked down, the façades of both Woolworth buildings are more in keeping with their surroundings than some of the structures erected in Hitchin in the following decades.

In 1841, Pierson's, a Hitchin bank, failed, and many of Hitchin's citizens lost money. Pierson's had occupied premises in the High Street, and the Quaker bank of Sharples, Exton and Lucas bought the site. They erected a new building, now Barclays Bank. Over the next 65 years, some of Hitchin's leading Quakers served on the board of directors, amongst them James Hack Tuke and Frederick Seebohm. Tuke came from York, moving to Hitchin in 1852. He was a great humanitarian, and involved himself in the poverty and starvation in Ireland. After the Franco-Prussian War and the siege of Paris in 1870-1, he travelled to Paris on a mission of relief. The government of the day consulted him as an expert on such matters. Seebohm too was a Quaker, and an amateur historian of considerable repute. His publications included 'The English Village Community', 'The Tribal System in Wales', and 'Tribal Custom in Anglo-Saxon Law'. They were at the time highly acclaimed pieces of original historical research. Sharples, Exton and Lucas eventually merged with other financial houses to become Barclays Bank.

Pound Lane was so-named because the pound for stray animals was situated at its western end. In 1834, it was widened and re-named Broad Street, but a short time later, it became Brand Street, after Sir Thomas Brand, Member of Parliament for Hertfordshire.

HIGH STREET AND BRAND STREET

A number of civic buildings were laid down along the new road: two Town Halls, in 1840 and 1901, a Library in 1861 and a Post Office in 1904 - replacing the one in the Market Place. At the end of the road was the Quaker meetinghouse and burial ground, where the graves of many of Hitchin's leading citizens may still be found.

Photograph 81713, right, shows the High Street, looking north towards Bancroft. Next to the Cock Hotel is Sanders and Sons, wireless and motor suppliers, then Perks and Llewellyn - established in Hitchin in 1790. They described themselves as 'cultivators and distillers of lavender'. Products ranged from bath and face powders to vanishing cream, and from 'Dr Young's Tonic' to 'Bronkure'. The business closed in 1961, but Violet Lewis, the last proprietor, stored the fittings and a good deal of its contents. In 1990, the collection was installed in Hitchin Museum, where they form an interesting and historically important display.

Further down the street are two tailors, T W Hall and Hepworth's. Westminster Bank occupies the near corner with Brand Street, and Lloyds Bank the furthermost. On the opposite side of the road is the Three Horseshoes, now closed. The nature of the traffic has changed since the previous picture; the horse has given way to the motorcar and bicycle.

Next to the Arcade in the High Street (see H89066, right), Merrick's sells sweets and tobacco. David Grieg's, the butcher, erected the imposing building opposite Barclays Bank. Woolworth's has replaced Perks and Llewellyn and, at about this time, on the first floor of the building next door, Hitchin's got its first taste of the east - a Chinese restaurant. The Cock Hotel, though much reduced in size, still displays its golden cock sign. The High Street is now one-way. At the time, innovation was described as 'experimental'; it has been a lengthy experiment.

A Methodist Chapel stood on the north side of Brand Street until it was demolished to make way for Sainsbury's supermarket. The same project saw the end of the Dog public house, a great personal favourite. The sign showed a black spaniel, and they served delicious meat pies. The Post Office made way for Halford's, suppliers of cycles and motorists' spares and accessories. In the past Chalkley's had provided a similar service; they had a garage next door to the Dog, and a bicycle shop on the other side of the road, next door to the Post Office Pensions Department.

HIGH STREET AND BRAND STREET

Above: THE HIGH STREET
1929 81713

Right: THE HIGH STREET
C1965 H89066

HITCHIN

HIGH STREET AND BRAND STREET

Right: CHALKLEY'S CYCLES ADVERTISEMENT

Chalkley's in Brand Street supplied both cycles and 'the Locomobile' steam motorcar in 1902. This advertisement appeared in a handbook celebrating the coronation of Edward VII.

Below: BRAND STREET C1955 H89036

The large building, centre left, is the old Town Hall, with the Library and Mechanics' Institute to its left (now Council offices). The New Town Hall is opposite, but it is not visible in this picture. The Quaker burial ground is at the centre of the picture, beneath the banner advertising a sports display at Woodside. On the right-hand-side are Latchmore's grocers, the Dog, the Methodist Chapel, and the Post Office. Note the decorative chimneys, right.

CYCLES AND MOTORS.

JOHN T. CHALKLEY,

THE CYCLE AND MOTOR WORKS,

BRAND STREET, HITCHIN.

Machines of the very Highest Grade as well as those at Popular Prices.

Cycles as supplied by J. T. CHALKLEY
are ridden by Their Majesties

KING EDWARD VII.,

The Kings of Italy, Belgium and Greece;

Their Royal Highnesses The Prince and Princess of Wales;

The Duchess of Fife, Princess Victoria,

Princess Charles of Denmark, &c., &c.

JOHN T. CHALKLEY is Agent for the Celebrated Noiseless
"LOCOMOBILE" STEAM MOTOR CAR.

GOD SAVE THE KING!

HIGH STREET AND BRAND STREET

A LAVENDER FIELD, MOUNT PLEASANT 1901
46655

Perks and Llewellyn's Mount Pleasant lavender fields, on the western outskirts of Hitchin in 1901. The cottage visible in the woods was used by the firm as a trademark, and appeared on many of their advertisements.

PERKS & LLEWELLYN ADVERTISEMENT

Perks & Llewellyn were established in 1790. Hitchin was famous for its lavender.

QUEEN STREET AND ST MARY'S SQUARE

HITCHIN FROM WINDMILL HILL 1922 71891

QUEEN STREET AND ST MARY'S SQUARE

HITCHIN FROM WINDMILL HILL 1929 81720

This shows the view from Windmill Hill looking towards St Mary's Parish Church, centre right. There is no indication in this photograph of the dreadful conditions existing in the Queen Street area. In this view the demolition of the Queen Street slums has been completed, and construction of St Mary's Square has begun.

QUEEN STREET AND ST MARY'S SQUARE

THE RIVER 1931 84196

Here is the St Mary's Square development, looking south. The only change to this riverscape has been the installation of a fountain in the middle. The cottages in the background face onto Biggin Lane; they have all been demolished. The site became the market in 1973.

QUEEN STREET AND ST MARY'S SQUARE

Until the mid 19th century, Queen Street consisted of Back Street and Dead Street. When Queen Victoria visited the town, it was thought unfitting that she should be driven along Dead Street, and the new name was devised. Dead Street meant what it said: according to tradition, most or all of its inhabitants died during the plague of 1348-1349. Back Street is a common name in English towns, and usually indicates a minor road, often running behind or parallel to the High Street.

The area of Queen Street and St Mary's Square consisted of slums until the 1920s: conditions were appalling. In 1849, a family of seven shared a single room in Davis Alley, with no windows or ventilation; in Chapman's Yard a girl of sixteen shared a bed with her three brothers, the oldest of whom was eighteen. Hewitt's Yard housed 127 people, and was served by just three privies. Thirty years later, the Local Board of Health deemed one privy between two dwellings, which between them might house as many as twenty people, was adequate for hygiene. Sewage went into the gutter or the river, and even permeated the walls of The Biggin. The communal water supplies were often contaminated, and outbreaks of cholera and typhoid fever were all too common. Between 1850-52, a sewage system was laid beneath the bed of the River Hiz. The intentions were good, but the design and installation was not. Joints between the pipes sometimes gave way, and then either the river disappeared into the sewer, or the sewage fountained from the surface of the river. On one occasion, during a heavy storm, raw sewage backed-up to the water supply and emerged from Hitchin's taps.

THE RIVER 1931 84198

By 1931, the redevelopment of St Mary's Square was complete. The river to the east of the church has been widened and landscaped, and bridges built to the north and south of the Churchyard. Details of the slum clearance are recorded on the main steps leading to the square. The buildings on the right are warehouses belonging to the Bancroft grocer, W B Moss. The newly built brick churchyard cloisters are on the left.

QUEEN STREET AND ST MARY'S SQUARE

In 1924, an extensive slum clearance programme began, resulting in the demolition of 174 cottages and the relocation of their 637 inhabitants to new housing elsewhere in the town. Completed in 1930, St Mary's Square was intended to become a new centre for the town, but the plan was never quite realised. Nonetheless, considerable work was done to improve the appearance of the Hiz as it flowed past St Mary's Church.

In 1939, the Square was given over to the market on Tuesdays and Saturdays. The move was temporary; in 1973, the market moved to a new site near the Churchyard, and since then St Mary's Square has been a car park.

No mention of Queen Street would be complete without mention of a remarkable survival story. In 1990, the Hitchin British Schools' buildings were put up for sale, and, thanks to the dedication of a group of enthusiasts, the site was saved from demolition. The importance of the site soon came to light: the extensive buildings include the only complete Lancasterian schoolroom left in Britain. The Lancasterian system of education relied upon older children, called monitors, to teach and supervise younger pupils, allowing large numbers of children to be managed by a single teacher. The Hitchin British Schools' Trustees are also custodians on the Jill Grey Collection, relating to the history of elementary education. This internationally important collection consists of around 17,000 books, 10,000 photographs and post cards, 2,000 items of ephemera and 1,500 objects. The school is open to the public, and receives regular visits from schools wishing to give their pupils a taste of methods of education in the past.

THE MARKET C1965 H89087

The market on St Mary's Square in the 1960s. The church and cloisters are clearly visible in the background. Moss's warehouse has gone, and the land has become a car park. The white-faced building, to the right of the church, is the recently built Church House. Immediately behind the cloisters are the offices of Hawkins & Co, Solicitors, the second oldest law firm in the England, dating from 1591.

Hermitage Road and Walsworth Road

Above: HERMITAGE ROAD 1901 46642

In 1901, Hermitage Road was a pleasant, open avenue. The building on the left in view 46642, left, is the Hermitage, home of Frederick Seebohm; very little of it still remains. Windmill Hill is just visible in the background.

Right: HERMITAGE ROAD c1965 H89079

HERMITAGE ROAD 1929 81722

In this 1929 photograph the north side of Hermitage Road is now built up, while the south side remains partly undeveloped. Some of the glass from the Hermitage was incorporated into the windows of the building on the left.

HERMITAGE ROAD AND WALSWORTH ROAD

The wealthy banker, Frederick Seebohm, lived at the Hermitage in Bancroft, in 1874. It was a large, rambling house with extensive gardens. At that time, the route to the railway station at the northern end of the town was via Bancroft, Silver Street and Nightingale Road. In order to shorten the journey Seebohm gave land to the town for a new road, between Bancroft and Walsworth Road. Hermitage Road opened in July 1875. For Seebohm there was a disadvantage - part of his estate was cut off by the new road, and the increase in traffic would make it less convenient for him to reach the Dell, which he also owned, on the other side of Walsworth Road. His solution was simple: the River Hiz had to flow beneath the new road, so he made the necessary tunnel sufficiently high and wide, so that he could walk through it. He built a tunnel beneath Walsworth Road to reach the Dell as well.

HERMITAGE ROAD
C1955 H89023

By the 1950s, new buildings have begun to overshadow the road. Barker's timber yard occupies the low range of buildings on the right. Further up the street the Hermitage cinema with its imposing entrance, is still open for business.

HERMITAGE ROAD AND WALSWORTH ROAD

Above: WALSWORTH ROAD 1901 46641

Walsworth Road in 1901, at the junction with Whinbush Road and looking towards the station. The building on the left is a lodge forming part of the Hermitage estate. It is still there, but the thatch has been replaced with cedar shingles. Behind the trees stands St Luke's Home of Rest for the Sick and Infirm.

Right: WALSWORTH ROAD 1901 46640

Still Walsworth Road, still 1901, but a little closer to the station. The wall on the right was built from slag and clinker from local foundries. The entrance leads to the Reverend Gainsford's residence.

WALSWORTH ROAD 1922 71895

Walsworth Road again, this time in 1922 and at the junction with Highbury and Verulam Roads. The pub on the left is the Radcliffe Arms, named for the Delmé-Radcliffe family who lived in the Priory for more than 400 years. The awnings over the shop windows next door are more extensive than most modern ones. The railings far left surround the Sacred Heart Convent.

HERMITAGE ROAD AND WALSWORTH ROAD

HITCHIN

The view from near the top of Hermitage Road (see H89079, page 70-71) is about ten years later. Barkers and the Hermitage cinema have gone to make way for the new Post Office and an office block. The Georgian building at the end of the road in Bancroft is doomed too, to make way for a supermarket. The large, gabled building on the right houses Hermitage Ballroom, a dance hall that was, in its day, the starting place of many a romance. Woolley's Garage sold petrol from the ground floor, with the fuel pipes leading above the heads of pedestrians. Cave's American Bar and Restaurant is on the right of the picture.

Many years were to pass before each side of the new road became the retail area it is today. The north side was complete by the 1920s, but the south suffered building and rebuilding. Barker's woodyard buildings with their mock-Tudor façade had maintained a low skyline but the buildings that replaced them did not. The largest building on the south side was the Hermitage Cinema, which opened in 1932 and closed in 1963. Though large, it was at least distinctive.

From the top of Hermitage Road, Walsworth Road runs northwards to the station. Originally little more than a track leading to the hamlet of Walsworth, the road rapidly filled with housing, both for the wealthy and for the large number of men working on the railway. The Reverend George Gainsford, who had been curate at St Mary's for a time, returned to Hitchin in 1863, to administer to the spiritual needs of the area, and building a new church - St Saviour's. He stayed for 45 years.

73

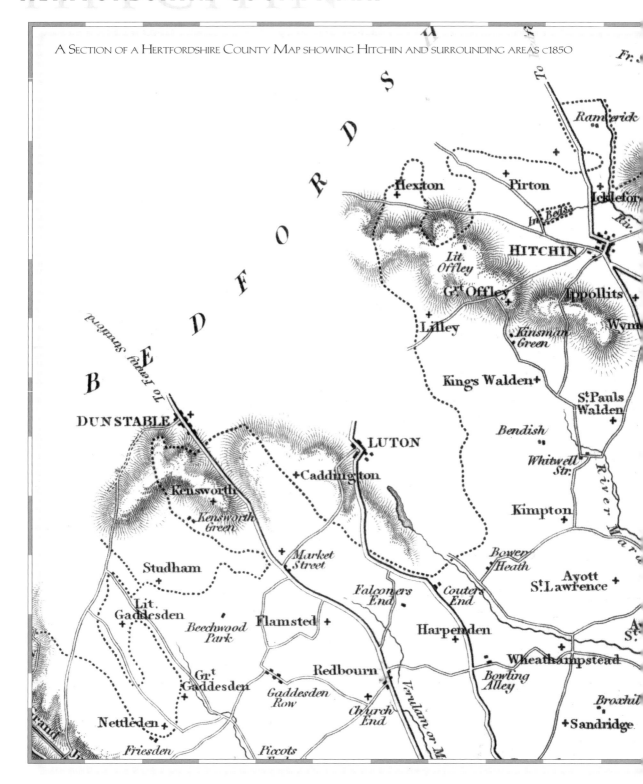

A Section of a Hertfordshire County Map showing Hitchin and surrounding areas c1850

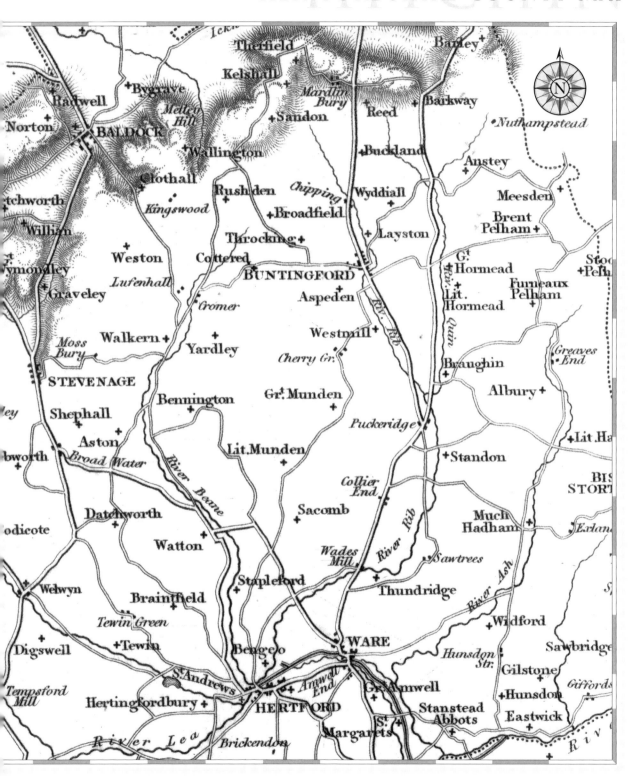

BANCROFT

BANCROFT

BANCROFT 1901 46637

B ancroft is a northward extension of the medieval High Street and, until 1903, it was the site of the livestock market in Hitchin.

Cattle, sheep and pigs were driven into town from all directions, causing mess and mayhem every market day. There had for some time been discussions about moving the livestock market, but it was not until a frightened cow tossed the Reverend Switzer's small son into the air that something happened. The Board of Agriculture stepped in, and new sites were leased or purchased, each side of Paynes Park. Local residents were delighted; their complaints about the noise and the obstruction of the road had in the past fallen upon deaf ears.

Following the closure of the market the nature of the street began to change, from predominantly residential, to the commercial and retail character of today.

Building styles range from late medieval to modern, with every period represented. Outstanding survivals include the Brotherhood House from the 15th century, the 17th-century Skinner's Almshouses, and the red brick police station of 1885. There are many others.

Photograph 46637, left, shows Bancroft, looking south in 1901. The building on the corner is W B Moss & Sons. It replaced the old Trooper Inn on the same site. The path to the left leads to the Churchyard. The area in front of the camera was the livestock market. Two of the granite posts on the right of the picture are still there.

Above: BANCROFT c1955 H89035

50 years later and Bancroft is on its way to becoming a busy shopping street. We last met Sanders in the High Street. Moss's are still on the corner bearing their name, and now have a second shop on the opposite side of the road. Two buildings further down is the Brotherhood House. Next to Blindell's is the Croft.

Right: BANCROFT c1955 H89015

Bancroft, looking north. It is 1955 and bicycles are everywhere. Motorcars are for the more affluent, though they are becoming more common.

Below: BANCROFT c1965 H89080

Bancroft in the mid to late 1960s, and hardly a bicycle in sight. The right turn is Portmill Lane, and when this picture was taken, the taxi rank was sited there. Compare this picture with the previous view.

THE CROFT 1929 81718

This building seems to have been preserved, but in fact, what exists today is a replica of the façade. Though altered over the years, parts of this old house dated from the 1400s. Though not ideal, its replacement is at least in keeping with the character of Bancroft.

BANCROFT, WILLIAM RANSOM BUILDINGS 1931 84206

The entrance to W Ransom and Sons' yard in 1931. This building is hardly changed - even the front door is the same after 70 years. The round brick chimneys are unusual. There seem to have been bargeboards on the gable, centre right, but little was left of them even then.

BANCROFT

Right: THE BOYS' GRAMMAR SCHOOL
1901 46643

The building on the left is the masters' boarding house.

Right: ST MICHAEL'S COLLEGE c1955
H89022

This Catholic school was established in Grove Road, close to the new Catholic Church on the corner of Nightingale Road.

BANCROFT

There is not room here to do more than glance at a few of Hitchin's schools, and the three selected are Hitchin Boys' School, Hitchin Girls' School and St Michael's College. Hitchin British School has already been mentioned.

Hitchin Boys' School was founded by John Mattocke as Hitchin Free School in 1632, and was originally located at the top of Tilehouse Street. After many years, it closed its doors in 1876, due to lack of funds. For over 20 years, a furious debate raged over its future. One faction wanted to re-open it as a grammar school, providing education for both boys and girls, while others thought that it should provide education for the poor. The grammar school supporters won and, in 1889, Hitchin Grammar School opened at Woodlands in Bancroft.

For some years, girls and boys were taught on the same site, though in different buildings; in 1908, extensive new premises were completed for the girls on Windmill Hill. At the Bancroft site, a new school hall was built in 1890, and a master's boarding house in 1901. Extensions followed, and the hall became the library. In 1974, the schools became a comprehensive.

St Michael's College was founded at the beginning of the 20th century. The original catholic school came from Mont Saint-Michel, fleeing anti-clerical laws in France. Over the next 65 years, St Michael's became a landmark in Grove Road, near to the Roman Catholic Church. In 1968, the school moved to Stevenage, and the Hitchin buildings made way for a police station.

THE GIRLS'
GRAMMAR
SCHOOL 1931
84211

This building allowed both grammar schools to expand.

Parks, Pleasure Grounds and Countryside

The people of Hitchin are fortunate in living in a rural district. Even today, open fields are within walking distance of every part of the town. In addition, there are playing fields, commons and parks within the town itself. Numerous footpaths and bridleways offer access to surrounding villages and towns.

DETAIL OF 84208

BANCROFT RECREATION GROUND 1931 84208

The pond has now been filled-in, due to concerns for children's safety. Behind the hut on the left is the bandstand.

Parks, Pleasure Grounds and Countryside

Priory Park 1901 46651

Extending to Charlton and beyond, the Park was owned by the Delmé-Radcliffe family for 400 years.

Oughton Head 1901 46658

The River Oughton rises from springs to the west of Hitchin, with its common land it still provides a pleasant riverside walk, as it did in 1901 when these photographs were taken.

Parks, Pleasure Grounds and Countryside

The View at West Mill 1901 46657

The Oughton flows to West Mill, feeding the millpond.

PARKS, PLEASURE GROUNDS AND COUNTRYSIDE

THE WATERFALL 1901 46656

At Westmill the Oughton falls from the millpond into the river course. There are at least three children peering from the bushes by the water.

Names of Subscribers

The following people have kindly supported this book by purchasing limited edition copies prior to publication.

Jean-Claude and Lydia Aka, Hitchin

K A and D J Barry, Hitchin

Marshall and Pat Baverstock

John Richard Beckwith

The Billingham Family, Hitchin

In Memory of Michael Biro

Mr C E Bishop and Mrs P M Bishop, Hitchin

Joanne and Roy Blyth, Preston, Hitchin

Eddie Bottoms, for his birthday, 2005

Stephen Bradford-Best

Amanda Brittany

David Burrows

Marc Burrows

Mr and Mrs J Burstow, Hitchin

John and Janet Creswell, née Newland, Peterbro'

Stephen Darnell

Diana and Philip Dawson, Reydon, Southwold

Elsie, Betty, Kate Day, for Emily, Ted and Brother Ted Day

Mrs E R Day, Hitchin

The Dolling Family, Hitchin

Dave and Anne Dunham, Poets Estate, Hitchin

John Edwards

Ender Family, June 2005, here since April 91

The Farrington Family, Hitchin

Joyce and David Fosdike, Golden Wedding

R Frohock, Hitchin

Kathleen Game

Nigel Victor Gilbert of Ickleford

John and Glenda Green, née Newland, Wellington

Brian and Sandra Haigh

Dr and Mrs Adrian Haigh

Barry, Valerie and Mark Hailey, Hitchin 2005

Bobbie and Robin Harwood

Mr C W Heyburn

D G B, Hitchin

Dennis and Sheila Holmes

G J R Homewood, Hitchin

John and Maureen Horton, Hitchin

John Hugill, Hitchin

T Husk, a wonderful man so sadly missed

To Peter Jackson on your 40th birthday

Sonia and Michael Kempson, Hitchin

The Kempson Family, Hitchin

In memory of George Kent, Hitchin

Betty Leverton, née Newland, Florida USA

M O Levy

The Lickfold Family, Hitchin

The Males Family of Symonds Road, Hitchin

Alan and Patricia Newbury, Hitchin

John and Laraine Newland, née Gray, Hitchin

Dennis Newlands, Hitchin

With love to my son, Keith Packwood

Mrs Mary S Page (née Cherry)

Mr M C and Mrs P Pascal, Hitchin

Eve Philpott, Hitchin

Mr R G and Mrs R P Pike, Hitchin

Mr J and Mrs B Pratchett, Hitchin

Dave Pridmore, on your 60th Birthday 03/06/05

In memory of A A Pettyfer, Hitchin

Mrs Ruth K Rawlings (née Cherry)

Mr and Mrs C A Roberts, Macclesfield

Penny, Roy, Jason and Kathy Scoot

The Pearman and Shepherd Families, Hitchin

Mr V J and L M T Smith, Hitchin

Darren and Graham Snowden, Hitchin

Brian Stocker, Hitchin

F C Stolborg and Family, Hitchin

Vic Summerfield, late of Hitchin

P C Swain, Hitchin

In memory of Linda Rosemary Tyler

The Wakefield Family, Hitchin

Graham Walton

Dr John and Mrs Jean Williams, Hitchin

For my parents Pat and Stan Wilmot 22/06/57

Charles and Pamela Wilson, Ickleford

In memory of Henry John Woodbridge

Mr and Mrs P R Young, Ickleford, Hitchin

INDEX

The Francis Frith Collection Titles

www.francisfrith.co.uk

The Francis Frith Collection publishes over 100 new titles each year. A selection of those currently available is listed below. For latest catalogue please contact The Francis Frith Collection. **Town Books** 96 pages, approximately 75 photos. **County and Themed Books** 128 pages, approximately 135 photos (unless specified).

Accrington Old and New
Alderley Edge and Wilmslow
Amersham, Chesham and Rickmansworth
Andover
Around Abergavenny
Around Alton
Aylesbury
Barnstaple
Bedford
Bedfordshire
Berkshire Living Memories
Berkshire Pocket Album
Blackpool Pocket Album
Bognor Regis
Bournemouth
Bradford
Bridgend
Bridport
Brighton and Hove
Bristol
Buckinghamshire
Calne Living Memories
Camberley Pocket Album
Canterbury Cathedral
Cardiff Old and New
Chatham and the Medway Towns
Chelmsford
Chepstow Then and Now
Cheshire
Cheshire Living Memories
Chester
Chesterfield
Chigwell
Christchurch
Churches of East Cornwall
Clevedon
Clitheroe
Corby Living Memories
Cornish Coast
Cornwall Living Memories
Cotswold Living Memories
Cotswold Pocket Album
Coulsdon, Chipstead and Woodmanstern
County Durham
Cromer, Sheringham and Holt
Dartmoor Pocket Album
Derby
Derbyshire
Derbyshire Living Memories
Devon
Devon Churches
Dorchester

Dorset Coast Pocket Album
Dorset Living Memories
Dorset Villages
Down the Dart
Down the Severn
Down the Thames
Dunmow, Thaxted and Finchingfield
Durham
East Anglia Pocket Album
East Devon
East Grinstead
Edinburgh
Ely and The Fens
Essex Pocket Album
Essex Second Selection
Essex: The London Boroughs
Exeter
Exmoor
Falmouth
Farnborough, Fleet and Aldershot
Folkestone
Frome
Furness and Cartmel Peninsulas
Glamorgan
Glasgow
Glastonbury
Gloucester
Gloucestershire
Greater Manchester
Guildford
Hailsham
Hampshire
Harrogate
Hastings and Bexhill
Haywards Heath Living Memories
Heads of the Valleys
Heart of Lancashire Pocket Album
Helston
Herefordshire
Horsham
Humberside Pocket Album
Huntingdon, St Neots and St Ives
Hythe, Romney Marsh and Ashford
Ilfracombe
Ipswich Pocket Album
Isle of Wight
Isle of Wight Living Memories
King's Lynn
Kingston upon Thames
Lake District Pocket Album
Lancashire Living Memories
Lancashire Villages

Available from your local bookshop or from the publisher

The Francis Frith Collection Titles (continued)

Lancaster, Morecambe and Heysham Pocket Album
Leeds Pocket Album
Leicester
Leicestershire
Lincolnshire Living Memoires
Lincolnshire Pocket Album
Liverpool and Merseyside
London Pocket Album
Ludlow
Maidenhead
Maidstone
Malmesbury
Manchester Pocket Album
Marlborough
Matlock
Merseyside Living Memories
Nantwich and Crewe
New Forest
Newbury Living Memories
Newquay to St Ives
North Devon Living Memories
North London
North Wales
North Yorkshire
Northamptonshire
Northumberland
Northwich
Nottingham
Nottinghamshire Pocket Album
Oakham
Odiham Then and Now
Oxford Pocket Album
Oxfordshire
Padstow
Pembrokeshire
Penzance
Petersfield Then and Now
Plymouth
Poole and Sandbanks
Preston Pocket Album
Ramsgate Old and New
Reading Pocket Album
Redditch Living Memories
Redhill to Reigate
Richmond
Ringwood
Rochdale
Romford Pocket Album
Salisbury Pocket Album
Scotland
Scottish Castles
Sevenoaks and Tonbridge
Sheffield and South Yorkshire Pocket Album
Shropshire
Somerset
South Devon Coast
South Devon Living Memories
South East London
Southampton Pocket Album
Southend Pocket Album
Southport

Southwold to Aldeburgh
Stourbridge Living Memories
Stratford upon Avon
Stroud
Suffolk
Suffolk Pocket Album
Surrey Living Memories
Sussex
Sutton
Swanage and Purbeck
Swansea Pocket Album
Swindon Living Memories
Taunton
Teignmouth
Tenby and Saundersfoot
Tiverton
Torbay
Truro
Uppingham
Villages of Kent
Villages of Surrey
Villages of Sussex Pocket Album
Wakefield and the Five Towns Living Memories
Warrington
Warwick
Warwickshire Pocket Album
Wellingborough Living Memories
Wells
Welsh Castles
West Midlands Pocket Album
West Wiltshire Towns
West Yorkshire
Weston-super-Mare
Weymouth
Widnes and Runcorn
Wiltshire Churches
Wiltshire Living Memories
Wiltshire Pocket Album
Wimborne
Winchester Pocket Album
Windermere
Windsor
Wirral
Wokingham and Bracknell
Woodbridge
Worcester
Worcestershire
Worcestershire Living Memories
Wyre Forest
York Pocket Album
Yorkshire
Yorkshire Coastal Memories
Yorkshire Dales
Yorkshire Revisited

See Frith books on the internet at www.francisfrith.co.uk

Frith Products & Services

Francis Frith would doubtless be pleased to know that the pioneering publishing venture he started in 1860 still continues today. Over a hundred and forty years later, The Francis Frith Collection continues in the same innovative tradition and is now one of the foremost publishers of vintage photographs in the world. Some of the current activities include:

Interior Decoration

Today Frith's photographs can be seen framed and as giant wall murals in thousands of pubs, restaurants, hotels, banks, retail stores and other public buildings throughout the country. In every case they enhance the unique local atmosphere of the places they depict and provide reminders of gentler days in an increasingly busy and frenetic world.

Product Promotions

Frith products are used by many major companies to promote the sales of their own products or to reinforce their own history and heritage. Frith promotions have been used by Hovis bread, Courage beers, Scots Porage Oats, Colman's mustard, Cadbury's foods, Mellow Birds coffee, Dunhill pipe tobacco, Guinness, and Bulmer's Cider.

Genealogy and Family History

As the interest in family history and roots grows world-wide, more and more people are turning to Frith's photographs of Great Britain for images of the towns, villages and streets where their ancestors lived; and, of course, photographs of the churches and chapels where their ancestors were christened, married and buried are an essential part of every genealogy tree and family album.

Frith Products

All Frith photographs are available Framed or just as Mounted Prints and Posters (size 23 x 16 inches). These may be ordered from the address below. From time to time other products - Address Books, Calendars, Table Mats, etc - are available.

The Internet

Already ninety thousand Frith photographs can be viewed and purchased on the internet through the Frith websites and a myriad of partner sites.

For more detailed information on Frith companies and products, look at these sites:

www.francisfrith.co.uk
www.francisfrith.com
(for North American visitors)

See the complete list of Frith Books at:

www.francisfrith.co.uk

This web site is regularly updated with the latest list of publications from The Francis Frith Collection. If you wish to buy books relating to another part of the country that your local bookshop does not stock, you may purchase on-line.

For further information, trade, or author enquiries please contact us at the address below:
The Francis Frith Collection, Frith's Barn, Teffont, Salisbury, Wiltshire, England SP3 5QP.
Tel: +44 (0)1722 716 376 Fax: +44 (0)1722 716 881   Email: sales@francisfrith.co.uk

---

See Frith books on the internet at www.francisfrith.co.uk

FREE PRINT OF YOUR CHOICE

Mounted Print
Overall size 14 x 11 inches (355 x 280mm)

Choose any Frith photograph in this book.
Simply complete the Voucher opposite and return it with your remittance for £2.25 (to cover postage and handling) and we will print the photograph of your choice in SEPIA (size 11 x 8 inches) and supply it in a cream mount with a burgundy rule line (overall size 14 x 11 inches).
Please note: **photographs with a reference number starting with a "Z" are not Frith photographs and cannot be supplied under this offer.**
Offer valid for delivery to one UK address only.

PLUS: Order additional Mounted Prints at HALF PRICE - £7.49 each (normally £14.99)
If you would like to order more Frith prints from this book, possibly as gifts for friends and family, you can buy them at half price (with no additional postage and handling costs).

PLUS: Have your Mounted Prints framed
For an extra £14.95 per print you can have your mounted print(s) framed in an elegant polished wood and gilt moulding, overall size 16 x 13 inches (no additional postage and handling required).

IMPORTANT!

These special prices are only available if you use this form to order . You must use the ORIGINAL VOUCHER on this page (no copies permitted). We can only despatch to one UK address. This offer cannot be combined with any other offer.

Send completed Voucher form to:
The Francis Frith Collection, Frith's Barn, Teffont, Salisbury, Wiltshire SP3 5QP

CHOOSE A PHOTOGRAPH FROM THIS BOOK

Voucher for **FREE** *and Reduced Price Frith Prints*

Please do not photocopy this voucher. Only the original is valid, so please fill it in, cut it out and return it to us with your order.

Picture ref no	Page no	Qty	Mounted @ £7.49	Framed + £14.95	Total Cost £
		1	Free of charge*	£	£
			£7.49	£	£
			£7.49	£	£
			£7.49	£	£
			£7.49	£	£
			£7.49	£	£
Please allow 28 days for delivery.			* Post & handling		£2.25
Offer available to one UK address only			**Total Order Cost**		£

Title of this book . . . .

I enclose a cheque/postal order for £ . . . .
made payable to 'The Francis Frith Collection'

OR please debit my Mastercard / Visa / Maestro / Amex card, details below

Card Number

Issue No (Maestro only)   Valid from (Maestro)

Expires   Signature

Name Mr/Mrs/Ms . . . .
Address . . . .
. . . .
. . . .
. . . . Postcode . . . .
Daytime Tel No . . . .
Email . . . .

ISBN 1-84589-0v 41-8   Valid to 31/12/08

Free Print – see overleaf

Can you help us with information about any of the Frith photographs in this book?

We are gradually compiling an historical record for each of the photographs in the Frith archive. It is always fascinating to find out the names of the people shown in the pictures, as well as insights into the shops, buildings and other features depicted.

If you recognize anyone in the photographs in this book, or if you have information not already included in the author's caption, do let us know. We would love to hear from you, and will try to publish it in future books or articles.

Our production team

Frith books are produced by a small dedicated team at offices in the converted Grade II listed 18th-century barn at Teffont near Salisbury, illustrated above. Most have worked with the Frith Collection for many years. All have in common one quality: they have a passion for the Frith Collection. The team is constantly expanding, but currently includes:

Paul Baron, Jason Buck, John Buck, Ruth Butler, Heather Crisp, David Davies, Louis du Mont, Isobel Hall, Lucy Hart, Julian Hight, Peter Horne, James Kinnear, Karen Kinnear, Tina Leary, Stuart Login, Sue Molloy, Sarah Roberts, Kate Rotondetto, Dean Scource, Eliza Sackett, Terence Sackett, Sandra Sampson, Adrian Sanders, Sandra Sanger, Julia Skinner, Miles Smith, Lewis Taylor, Shelley Tolcher, Lorraine Tuck, Miranda Tunnicliffe, David Turner and Ricky Williams.